MW00607018

Tips and Techniques
For First Time Teachers

by

Diana Skoog

with

Mary Peirce Bale

◆ ◆ ◆

Mother's House Publishing
Colorado Springs, CO

© 2009 Diana Skoog Colorado Springs, CO
All rights reserved.

Illustrations by Alan Lee Bale and Agnes Madrill Reininger
Author photograph by Sears Photo Studio

Chapters that describe national programs are included to inform the reader about that particular process and are written from personal notes by the author obtained through attending workshops. They are intended not to replace individual research but to give a comprehensive overview and to encourage the interested party in attending a workshop of their own.

The teaching tips and techniques in this book are the personal experience of the author and are presented to encourage the first time teacher in gaining confidence in the classroom. It is assumed that the readers will use their own good judgment in choosing and applying what is practical and useful in any particular situation or classroom. The author makes no claim as a therapist or medical practitioner of any kind but does wish you the good fortune of excellent first years!

Published by
Mother's House Publishing
2814 East Woodmen Road
Colorado Springs, CO 80920
719-266-0437 / 800-266- 0999
info@mothershousepublishing.com
www.mothershousepublishing.

Printed and bound in Colorado Springs, CO
Made in the United States of America

ISBN 978-1-935086-45-1
ISBN 1-935086-45-6

To schedule Diana for a presentation, contact her at:
Diana@sskoog.com.

This book is well organized, simple to read and understand. The topics covered are those that teachers confront daily but may not have been covered in their college courses.

This book will be a valuable resource to new as well as seasoned teachers. It's a great "top desk drawer" handbook. Well done!

T. S., Elementary school teacher, Lincoln, Nebraska

Each chapter offered great information such as: Hands on knowledge pertaining to the characteristics of underachievers in Chapter III, discipline and dignity method explained in Chapter IV, Chapter VIII on oral presentations that include delivery techniques is very valued, and the VAT Teaching concept covered in Chapter IX is an important concept to understand.

K. F. Elementary school teacher.

Diana included lots of helpful hints; things new teachers may not know. Diana gives new teachers a "head start" in the field of teaching. There is lots of helpful information given in Chapter I. Chapter II introduces great ways for students to get to know each other. In Chapter VI, the Sentence formation/structure suggests a great way for students to remember abstract concepts. Chapter IX covers VAT Teaching that is important to being an effective teacher!

I wish someone had put this kind of information into my hands before I began my first year of teaching. New teachers will be so blessed by your words of wisdom!

H. R., Teacher (taught with the author on the same teaching team)

This book contains a very good collection of things that first time teachers should understand and know how to do. It contains many well-thought-out concepts and methods that cannot be learned in one reading, but when really practiced, will definitely result in more successful teaching results. This work reflects excellent understanding of the topic area and details.

The book addresses the relationship between teacher and students, to include verbal and visible communication between them. It suggests specific detailed techniques that can be practiced until they become habits for successful learning outcomes.

Melvin J. Anderson, Ph.D.

Acknowledgements

I have so many people to thank for their contributions to this book.

First, I must thank Mary Peirce Bale who worked tirelessly with me, filling in with typing and word choice the holes of organization with which my brain injury had left me.

Second, I want to thank my husband Steve, who regularly brought me notepads to use since I use paper like water. He faithfully gave me encouragement, support, and editing assistance — whether I wanted it or not!

Thanks to my two children, Joshua and Stephanie, who willingly (if not happily) gave up the computer when Mom needed to write.

The ability to pursue this dream comes thanks to the skill of Dr. Michael Brown of Colorado Springs Neurological Associates, whose surgical skill brought me through my AVM crisis.

Additionally, I want to thank my publisher, Jackie Haag, without whose encouragement this book would not have been finished.

Dr. Jean Bressler, my advisor at the College of Education at the University of Nebraska at Omaha (UNO) in the beginning of my teaching career, gave me much guidance and encouragement with which to start teaching on the right foot.

Also, I benefited greatly from the many wonderful teachers with whom I taught over the years, especially those at Challenger Middle School, Colorado Springs, Colorado, who renewed my confidence in teaching after a frustrating previous year. Also, I benefited from my supervisors who were truly interested in my career and helped me become a better teacher.

Finally, I gained much insight from my students. They tolerated my constant growth and taught me the importance of caring both for them and for my subject area and for helping me to see the necessity of making each course relevant to real life experience.

And last but most important of all, I thank God, who allowed me to retain my writing ability when most other abilities were gone.

Diana Skoog

Foreword

It has been an eye-opening and rewarding experience to work with Diana on this education guide for first time teachers. Diana was in the middle of her teaching career when she suffered a cerebral event that left her in a coma and its successive states for over seven months. Somehow, miraculously, she gradually woke up from the coma but then she had to face the reality of how this trauma had ravaged her body and to discover her physical limitations.

With the tender care and devotion of her husband, Steve, Diana worked through the hours, days, and months of rehabilitation for her mind and body.   The support of her children, Joshua and Stephanie, along with extended family and friends, has enabled Diana to regain a workable life. Shortly after I met Diana, I discovered she had produced quite a body of written work in several genres. They include poetry, stories, songs, and non-fiction. I suspect writing has been Diana's own special therapy and a way for her to express her true self.

Diana attended the University of Nebraska at Omaha. She earned a BS Degree in Secondary Education with majors in Language Arts and Speech Communication. She held a teaching certificate in Nebraska and has a teaching license in Colorado. Diana taught Secondary English/Language Arts for 15 years in Colorado Springs. During her career she had gained much experience and insight into the world of teaching and in dealing with students, gifted students, and underachievers. First time teachers would seek her out and ask for guidance and information on

how to work more effectively with students.

Diana decided to produce a book of tips, techniques, and concepts for teachers that she learned over the years and share the knowledge she had collected in that time. In addition, this book has been a way for her to share the joy she experienced in her teaching career and to continue to contribute to the educational field that she dearly loves.

Through this book, *Tips and Techniques for First Time Teachers*, Diana hopes to provide valuable information and guidance for new teachers as they start their own careers. The knowledge she has acquired will greatly assist first time teachers and enable them to help their students achieve their educational goals in very productive ways.

Mary Peirce Bale

Introduction

I taught Secondary English/Language Arts in the Colorado Springs area for 15 years until 1998, when I suffered a brain aneurysm and stroke, which resulted in a disability retirement. During the time I was teaching, I gained much information beyond what I learned in my college classes, from other teachers, my supervisors, and several workshops I attended. All these were my resources for this book. I felt it would be a crime for all of that experience and information to go unused. In addition to this, I had several friends who joined the teaching profession and asked me for tips due to (or maybe in spite of ☺) my years of experience.

Consequently, I felt there might be a need for this information compiled into an informational guidebook. I know I certainly would have appreciated a guidebook like this before my first year of teaching. My first teaching position was at a small school where there were no departments or teams to provide help or ideas. In fact, I was the entire 9-12 English department! Nevertheless, I had a good year!

It was there that I saw the words on a plaque that would guide a large part of my teaching career. They were, "Students don't care what you know until they know that you care." Additionally, I heard a speaker at a conference make the observation that, "Yours may be the only smile that students see that day." Both of these made a great impression upon me.

In spite of feeling a little isolated at times, I loved my new profession and I persevered and taught for eight more years before I suffered the career ending aneurysm. Finding my way back, with the significant help of my family, created a different set of obstacles and a new standard for recording achievements!

Obviously, in the years before the accident, the first thing I learned was how to start each year/class. This I gained from trial and error and the many wonderful teachers with whom I taught. I now offer them to you. May your first year, and every subsequent year, be filled with purpose and a joyful teaching experience.

Time Line

1983...............Graduated from University of Nebraska-Omaha

1983-84............Substituted in schools in the Colorado Springs area.

1984-89............Peyton High School 9-12 English and Speech
Communication.

1990-92............Lewis-Palmer High School 9-10 English

1993-95............Immanuel and Redeemer Lutheran Schools 6-8
Language Arts.

1996-97............Challenger Middle School sixth grade
Language Arts

1997-98............Eagleview Middle School seventh grade
Language Arts

1998...............Air Academy High School tenth grade English

September 23, 1998 Suffered Arterio-Venous Malformation stroke

December 1998.........Spoke for the first time since event

April 1999..............Went home from the third hospital

Over time, these were the next accomplishments:

- Trip to Disney World & Daytona Beach
- Voice lessons to regain speaking and singing strength
- Sang in four recitals (albeit very softly)
- Participated in church's praise band/worship team (what she may have lacked in pitch or volume was overcome by the joy in her face and hand motions, and playing of the [musical] dolphin)
- Sang in a fifties performing group
- Operates lights for husband's classic rock band, *Coyote*
- Worked on the team that helped conduct 3 retreats.
- Presented at Via de Cristo (Lutheran Cursillo) retreats
- Wrote 4 devotionals for church's Lenten devotional book
- Wrote puppet show script for day care center.
- 25th wedding anniversary trip to Kauai

April 2009...............Published my first book!

Table of Contents

CHAPTER 1: FIRST DAY FOUNDATIONS Starting Your Year/ClassRight 1

    Getting Acquainted 3

    Establishing Expectations 4

    Classroom Policies... 5

    Let Them Get to Know You 6

    Topics to Discuss 7

CHAPTER 2: FINDING FRIENDLY FACTS Getting Acquainted With Your Students.. 9

    Index Cards 9

    Filing the Index Cards... 11

    90-Second Life Story 12

    Interview/Questionnaire and Introduction to the Class 12

    Presenting Introductions 14

CHAPTER 3: UNDERSTANDING UNDERACHIEVEMENT Helping those students who have problems performing to their ability 15

    Definition 18

    Causes 18

    Deterring Perfectionism in the Classroom. 18

    Identifying Underachievers' Characteristics 19

    Tools Available to Identify Underachievers 19

    Characteristics of Underachievers 19

    Two Types of Underachievers 20

    Causes of Underachievement.. 22

    Reversing the Problem 23

CHAPTER 4: LOVE AND LOGIC LESSONS Disciplining with dignity for both you and your students 33

    Effective Classroom Management....................................... 33

    Self–Concept:.. 34

    Hierarchy of Problem Solving 34

    Control 35

Consequences.. 35

CHAPTER 5: MORE MATERIAL Additional skills you can teach outside of your subject area:writing, speaking, and study skills......... 37

OralPresentations 37

StudySkills 37

NoteTaking 38

Collaborate with Other Subject Areas 39

Time Management Skills 40

CHAPTER 6: CREATING COOPERATIVE COMMUNITIES Creative ways to form small groups with rules, activities, and assignmentideas 43

Popsiclesticks 43

PlayingCards 44

Clothing... 44

TextbookNumbers.. 45

Names 45

Rules for Small Group Activities.. 45

Projects Outside of School 47

Large Group Activities 47

Types of Activities 47

Sentence Formation Structure 48

Barrel of Monkeys 49

CHAPTER 7: CLASSROOM AIDES Using help as efficiently as possible 51

Non Academic Help.. 51

Miscellaneous Classroom Contributions 52

Help in Academic Areas 53

FindingAides.. 54

CHAPTER 8: ORAL PRESENTATIONS Easy delivery techniques you can teach your students for class and for "real life situations" 55

DeliveryTechniques 56

CHAPTER 9: VAT TEACHING Teaching to different learning styles (Visual, Auditory, and Tactile Learners) 59

VisualLearners 60

AuditoryLearners 60

TactileLearners 61

Identifying Learning Styles.. 63

CHAPTER 10: HANDLING THE PAPER LOAD Alternatives to detailed grading when faced with that mountain of papers you need to grade.. 65

Packets 65

Checklists.. 66

Techniques for Grading Writing Assignments 66

Six-Trait Writing Skills.. 67

CHAPTER 11: OCCUPYING OPENERS Techniques for starting a class that will allow you to complete those tasks which are necessary for beginning the class 69

"Mod minutes" (Modification Examples)...................... 69

SSR (Sustained Silent Reading)..................................... 70

Journal/Log 70

CHAPTER 12: CONFIDENCE THROUGH COMPETITION Helping students find their comfort zone 73

CHAPTER 13: ACCOUNTABILITY Teaching students how to be responsible and getting them to take responsibility for their choices. 77

CHAPTER 14: FINAL TIPS 85

Banking.. 85

Games 88

Free Late Homework Coupon... 91

Good Deed Notification Forms....................................... 92

Treasure Chest/Privilege Coupons................................. 94

ProblemSolving.. 97

Absences 98

Appendix I: Weekly Evaluation Form 99

Appendix II: Nine Famous People Who Blew It (But Later Made It Big) 100

Appendix III: General Notes and Hints from a Fifteen-year Veteran Teacher... 102

Appendix IV: Extra-Curricular Experience 106

Appendix V: Evaluation for Five Traits of Public Speaking........... 108

Conclusion 110

CHAPTER 1: FIRST DAY FOUNDATIONS
Starting Your Year/Class Right

Students don't care what you know until they know that you care.
Anonymous

My first experience in getting acquainted with my students was anything but ordinary. When I walked into the classroom filled with seniors at my first school, I immediately found myself face to face with the school's popular heavyweight wrestler who promptly pointed his first two fingers toward my face and said, "Watch out or I'll poke your eyes out!" Refusing to be intimidated and sensing that he was just trying to show off, I imitated his words and gesture saying, "You better pay attention or I'll poke your eyes out!" I never had a problem with him the rest of the year. As time progressed I found him to be a strong class leader. I was never sure if the class was afraid of him or just respected him, but I came to appreciate his contributions to the classroom.

In addition to that experience in getting to know my students, I also had an automatic agenda for the first day. Since this was my first teaching experience, I had gone to the school a couple of weeks before the first day to get acquainted with my classroom and textbooks. It was then that I discovered there were no literature books and the grammar book was not marked clearly with the proper grade level. Since I was the entire nine through twelve English Department, I had to determine this for myself. I knew nothing about the textbook, not to mention the students' knowledge. It seemed necessary to learn each of these pieces of information at the same time. Luckily, as I scanned the textbooks, I noticed a pre-test that I could use to establish the student's knowledge level. That became a necessary part of the first day activities. This also gave me a good feel for which textbook would be appropriate for each grade level.

The next part of first day activities was getting to know the school rules and requirements. Since I was new not only to the school but to teaching in general, I had no knowledge of how any school handled those things. My solution involved having the advantage of beginning with the senior class, most of whom had experience with the set up of the school. Lacking any written student handbook, I utilized the students' knowledge in that area to prepare me for the other grades. The seniors felt valued with their input in this area. Obviously the freshmen class was as clueless as I, so we started on the same level. My revelation to them resulted in an animated discussion about what they thought the rules might be.

In addition to my getting acquainted with the students and all of us getting acquainted with the school, the students needed to learn *my* rules and expectations. I provided them with a reference list of these guidelines for their daily use. I also requested that they take the list home for their parents to review and sign. This way I knew the parents were aware of my rules and expectation in case a future problem arose. I had the students keep the signed rules in their notebook or folder. If there was a breach in following the rules I could say, "What was the rule about that issue?" or, "Lets review the rule."

Here is a guideline that may be of help to you as you establish the dynamic of your new year. Most can be remembered by the acronym PRE: Policies, Rules, and Expectations.

Getting Acquainted

Choose one of the ideas in Chapter Two which you'd like to follow, or create one of your own. It is important to let students know you are authentically interested in learning about them and letting them know that you care.

Establishing Expectations

Let students know what you expect from them for complete sentences and assignment headings such as class period, block number, name, date, assignment, or page numbers.

You should also inform your students how you will handle work turned in without a name. Believe it or not, this will happen. One idea to limit problems in this area that I adopted was to put all unnamed work in a "recycle" bin from which students could claim their work *before* it was graded. I chose this as one of the rules when I discovered that some students would try to claim the paper with the highest grade as their own. Now who would do a thing like that?

Tell your students what materials you expect them to bring to class every day:

~ Spiral or binder for use in your class only.
~ A book for leisure reading in addition to the textbook. (Sometimes I would allow students to read if they finished a test before the rest of the class.)
~ Writing utensils and highlighters for notes.

Tell your students your policy about late assignments and homework. Some ideas I have used are:

~ Late is not accepted at all.
~ 10 points deducted for each day late.

~ A "free homework" coupon, accepted once per quarter. To assist me in keeping track of this practice, I would paperclip all work I collected on the due date and attach a sticky note to the stack indicating what the assignment was, period or block number, and date collected. Then, when I graded them, if any assignment was missing I would mark my grade book so I would know if it had later been turned in. When the assignment was turned in, I'd write "in" plus "the date" at the top of the late assignment.

You could give the free homework coupons for a variety of reasons: at the beginning of each quarter, earned for no missing work for a predetermined time, or special days like Christmas, Valentine's Day, birthdays, and so forth.

Classroom Policies

Review or explain you team or school's policy on book returns at the end of the year, including book condition and payment for damage.

Review or explain your school's policy about missed homework for absences and required time for make-up work. If your school does not have, one it might be good to suggest that your department or team establish one that all would support.

Review or explain your department or the school's Student Handbook, including dress code.

Establish or explain your classroom rules about behavior and type of writing utensils allowed. This may seem silly, but I found I had to outlaw yellow pens because they were too hard to read, and I had to outlaw any color I might use for grading. In a math class, this may be especially important when considering erasure. In other classes, you may not want them to erase at all.

Explain classroom supply needs. If you are going to require a journal or other accumulation of notes, they will need a separate spiral for your class and possibly a steno style book for notes.

At this time, it is also a good idea to explain your expectations for material they are to bring to class each day.

Review or establish your rules or the school's about cell phones and ear piece music in your classroom.

If you have a computer in your classroom, you will need to explain rules for use and even rules for being around them.

Discuss rules and preferences about food or drinks and chewing gum in your classroom. You may also want to address the issue of wearing sunglasses in your room. I always emphasized the fact that eye contact is an important aspect of communication and that it gives me feedback about their understanding.

Let Them Get to Know You

I always gave them the same information I had asked from them, preferably in the same format, although as you will find as you explore these options in Chapter Two, an index card is a little hard to pass around.

Let them know how you would prefer to be approached about grades, missing homework and work missed when absent. The "Love and Logic" approach, which you may or may not want to adopt, states that the student needs to solve his own problem in any way that doesn't cause a problem for anyone else, including you.

Let your students know your policy for "posting" grades, when and how they can learn current grades and missing assignments, etc. Between standard grading periods, some schools may have strict rules about posting grades for privacy reasons. Therefore, it is advisable to check with your principal before telling students how you will do this.

Topics to Discuss

Discuss the syllabus and overall content of the class.

Discuss your grading plans and procedures for tests and assignments.

Discuss the contents of the textbook and how they can best utilize it, i.e. presence and location of a glossary.

Discuss any important terms that are specific to your subject area that might be helpful to know as they start studying this subject. This is especially important in math and science, but valuable in all areas. Obviously, you do not want to be redundant and cover terms that are explained in the first chapter.

Notes

CHAPTER 2: FINDING FRIENDLY FACTS
Getting Acquainted With Your Students

*"One hundred years from now
It will not matter what kind of car I
drove, what kind of house I lived
in, how much money I had in my
bank account, nor what my clothes
looked like. But one hundred years
from now the world may be a little
better because I was important in
the life of a child.*
~Dr. Forest E. Witcraft

One way to get acquainted is Questions. There is always the traditional method of circulating among the students and asking questions to gain information, but I could never remember the answers, so I searched for other more interesting and *recordable* ideas.

Index Cards

Hand out an index card to each student. Ask your students to fill out the information you would like to know. Some possibilities are as follows. Assure the students that the information obtained will be strictly confidential, and then insure that it is.

a. Name - you may want this at the top of the card for filing purposes, and in "last name first" format.

b. Period or Block number.

c. Textbook number - I asked students to take the card and textbook home and look over the book with their parents and mark on the back of the card any significant damage they find, having their parents sign under that. This establishes that the parents know the condition of the book when it was assigned to the student and, in addition, you will have the same information. To encourage prompt return of the card and its completion, I offered a small number of extra credit points if it was returned, signed, by the next day.

d. Some ideas for additional information on the card are as follows

> Extra curricular activities
> Sports, clubs, etc. Anything major that
>   may have a scheduling influence on their time
> Test or major project due-dates
> Ideas for future writing topics
> Ideas about topics of interest so that I
>   could simply to get to know them
> Hobbies (for the same reasons as above)
> Any other family information which may
>   influence homework completion
> Dual custody between split parents, as I
>   learned that this affects students
>   concerning when they are able to do

homework, location of textbook, etc.
Information about an ill or disabled
parent or sibling, and personal health
issues which may affect the students
ability to do homework.

It is important to let your students know you are interested in learning who they are and that you consider such information when making assignments, setting due dates, and so forth. Too often students feel they have no control over anything that happens in school and thus fight against being told what to do and when to do it. I did try to avoid certain dates for major assignments or tests, especially when I had several students in the same activity, such as State Championship games, drama performances, or band concerts.

Filing the Index Cards

The most common way of keeping track of these cards is to find a locking box to file them in. I found out by accident that a wooden cigar box is the perfect size, or a recipe box can also work. Another useful way I employed this idea was to substitute the cards with file folders. I would give each student a file folder on the first day, have them write their name on the tab, last name first, and asked them to decorate it in any way they wished, but that their parents would be seeing the folders. Then I would collect and keep them in a locking file cabinet drawer where I would use the folders to hold their papers, tests, essays, or any writing projects of quality. I found this to be helpful at parent teacher conference time when I needed to have the students' work to show parents.

90-Second Life Story
(My personal favorite)

Tell students they will be telling their group their life story in 90 seconds, so they should be thinking about what they would like to say.

Divide students into groups of five or six apiece. Brainstorm with the class or in the groups about the types of information you would like them to include in their stories.

Begin with any person in the group and give them 90 seconds to tell their life story to the rest of their group in whatever way they wish. Then move around the group giving each student 90 seconds to tell his story

You will find that even if you do not brainstorm first, the students will cover most of the important information and will even adopt some information topics from the previous student. However, there may be some information omitted that you would like them to have shared.

This activity also serves as an activity for them to gain trust in each other so they are more willing to work in small groups in the future.

Interview/Questionnaire and Introduction to the Class

This is very similar to 90-Second Life Story, but has a slightly different approach, one with which some students

may be more comfortable. It also gives students a chance to get their feet wet in giving an oral presentation.

Create a questionnaire containing the information, such as that in the 90-Second Life Story that you would like to know.

Divide students into groups of a size that fit your facilities and time. Within the groups, pair students in whatever way you would like, or allow them to choose their own partner. Tell students they will be introducing to the class the student they interview.

It might be a good opportunity to pair a new student with one who has been at the school awhile.

Give them an appropriate amount of time to complete the interview. Five minutes is usually adequate

They could choose the way they would like to use the questionnaire or you can decide for them. The pairs could have the interviewee fill it out and then the interviewer can use the form for the introduction, or you can instruct them to have the interviewer fill out the questionnaire as they ask the questions. This latter method is better in that the interviewer will get to know the person and can remember the information easier when speaking to the class.

To create the subsequent pairs you may wish to use this method: the interviewer becomes the person to the right of the previous one; the interviewee becomes the person to their left or opposite them in the group. You can keep

moving around the group in this way until you are ready to begin the introductions.

Presenting Introductions

Have each interviewer tell the class about their interviewee. Encourage them to give an introduction and conclusion to their talk just as they would if writing an essay about them.

To add an unexpected twist to the onset of the presentations, ask a student to raise his or her hand and then have the student to that person's right be the first one to present.

If you want to insure good listening by the rest of the class, you could hand out duplicates of the questionnaire to the class and ask them to fill it out about one of the interviewees as they listen to the talks.

Tell them to be certain to put the interviewees name on their form.

This could be graded for accuracy or simply for completion.

CHAPTER 3: UNDERSTANDING UNDERACHIEVEMENT
Helping those students who have problems performing to their ability

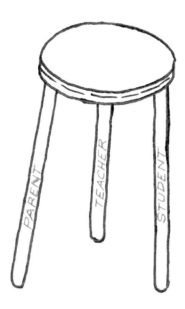

The reason I pursued this topic was two-fold. First, my own son was struggling with a problem in his third grade class. From the time he was a toddler I had recognized that he was an auditory learner. I also knew he hated repetitive activities. I did not know, however, what was causing him to be in danger of failing third grade. Secondly, I was struggling with some of my own students not turning in homework and thus being in danger of failing my class. Nothing I tried seemed to help. It was at this time that I received a flyer about a class being offered by a local college for professional development called "Reversing Underachievement." Needing credits to keep current with renewing my state teaching license, I enrolled. I immediately recognized the definition and characteristics of underachievement given in the class as those exhibited by my son and several of my students. Needless to say, this was perhaps the most informative and useful class I ever took. In addition to that class, and probably because of it, I later received an invitation to attend a conference of the International Underachievement Institute. The conference was offered in Minnesota that summer, and given by Dr. Sylvia Rimm, PhD., a recognized authority on the subject. What I learned from those classes forms the basis of this chapter.

Unity

I dreamed I stood in a studio
And watched two sculptors there
They used a young child's mind
They fashioned it with care.
One was a teacher – the tools she used
Were books, music and art.
The other, a parent, worked with a guiding hand,
And a gentle loving heart.
Day after day, the teacher toiled
With touch that was deft and sure,
While the parent labored by her side
And polished and smoothed it o'er.
When at last the task was done,
They were proud of what they wrought,
The things they molded into the child
Could neither be sold or bought.
And each agreed they would have failed
If each had worked alone,
Behind the parent stood the school
And behind the teacher, the home.

Anonymous

Definition

Underachievement concerns a discrepancy between a child's school performance and some index of actual ability.

Causes

1. Lack of involvement with homework by dads. Since boys make up a larger percentage of this population, and since children identify with the same sex parent from about the age of 3, it is important that dads be involved in (monitoring) the homework. Boys may think that homework is not important for males. Unfortunately, peers who think that it is not "cool" for boys to be smart too often reinforce this.

2. Perfectionism. Whether by parents or the student, perfectionists often set unrealistic expectations for themselves and the student may feel that it is so impossible to live up to the expectations that it's not worth trying.

Deterring Perfectionism in the Classroom.

Tell them about famous people who failed, often several times, but went on to achieve greatness (see Appendix 1).

Teach goal setting, including small steps to meet them, and people and resources which might also be of assistance. Teach him to set realistic, attainable goals to achieve success.

Acknowledge you own imperfections and don't be afraid to admit when you don't know something or were wrong. For example, tell your student you will get back to him with the answer, or that in your desire to help him you made a mistake, which you will correct before the situation occurs again.

Identifying Underachievers' Characteristics

There are formal evaluation tools available, but most teachers can identify these students without investing additional time. Often a conference with the parents or counselor will accomplish the same thing.

Tools Available to Identify Underachievers

One of the tools that can be used to identify underachievers is called the AIM (Achievement Identification Measure); however, these are not always needed if you can hold an inclusive meeting with the important people involved in the success of the student.

Characteristics of Underachievers

1. Students who are sure they turned in an assignment, but claim that you lost it.

2. Easily distracted, daydream a lot.

3. Often dawdle when working in class.

4. Poor or no study and organization skills.

Two Types of Underachievers

1. Dominant

a. These students like to dominate the situation, and are reluctant to get involved in a situation they are not sure they can dominate.

b. They like to debate and argue over almost anything, especially if they think they can win.

c. Will finish work quickly, but they are more concerned with being done first than with the quality of their work.

d. At home some are lonely and withdrawn, while others are bossy and lose temper easily.

e. All are manipulative to some degree.

f. Will fail to turn in assignments on a regular basis, especially when they say they "can't find it." Some parents say they've seen the student complete it and don't understand why it didn't get turned in.

g. Poor organizational skills. They forget homework or lose it or misplace textbooks and notebooks.

When I became aware that my son was having a problem, I went to school and found several completed assignments stuffed in the bottom of his locker that were not graded, so I knew they had never been turned in. My son's comment was that he could not find them when it was time to hand them in. Small wonder ☺. Consequently, we began trying to find an organizational method that would work for him.

This proved to be much harder than I would have thought; the first lesson learned was that a method that worked for me would not necessarily work for him. I could understand this, but finding one that would work for him was difficult. We decided that a planner was essential, even for a third grader. Since my team had been utilizing them successfully at the middle school where I worked, I adopted the same practice with my son. This involved asking the teacher to initial the day's assignments in his planner so I would know those were, indeed, the assignments for that day. My son also had to write the due date next to each one. Then at home when he had completed each one, he could check it off, and when finished, I would sign at the bottom. The teacher would then know it had been completed. It was his responsibility to go to the teacher for the initials, and to show the teacher my signature at a convenient time.

As a teacher I kept a bag of small candies on hand and offered one to students who had completed planner entries for a full week, especially parent signatures.

2. Dependent

a. Quiet, pleasant

b. Manipulates adults by seeking help with their work.

c. Tends to cry and become easily frustrated.

d. Report headaches, stomachaches, and minor illnesses.

e. Tends to ask questions and has difficulty following directions.

f. In elementary school, they tend to complete work but the work may not be of good quality.

g. Does not like to write, it's "too hard".

h. Appear not as bright as they are.

Causes of Underachievement

Things that contribute/ predispose students toward underachievement:

1. Negative job talk: Encourage parents to talk positively around the student especially when discussing their jobs. If a student hears too much negative talk about the parents' jobs, they may feel that achievement is not valuable if it results in a job with so many hassles.

2. Too much help: As a teacher I had always believed that it was good to help (only help) my child with his homework to make sure he understood it. However, I came to learn that parents who help too much with homework may be unwittingly causing students to become too dependent on their help for completing it and the unconscious message is often perceived as "you can't do this yourself."

3. Too much of a good thing.

Another related cause is parents who are too complimentary.

I had always believed complimenting kids helped give them a positive self-image. It may also give them an inflated picture of their abilities and one which they may feel pressured to live up to.

Don't omit compliments, but try to compliment the effort rather than their personality. One very powerful way to compliment your student is to speak highly of your child when speaking to a third party, especially when your child is unaware that you know he is listening. Obviously, it is important that this be done subtly. This is known as "referential speaking."

4. Perfectionist attitudes on the part of the student or the parent. If parents expect perfection, the student may feel it is impossible to complete the homework to their standards, therefore, he may feel it is not worth the effort. A student with a perfectionist attitude has learned to demand too much, becoming dependent upon constant exclamations of excellence and admiration. They see crediting of other children's achievement and correction as condemnation to them. They tend to blame their family and school for their problems. They rebel against "establishment goals" and feel that opposition establishes their identity. They push limits and refuse to accept "no". They claim teachers do not like them. They like teachers to give them special privileges and feel out of control unless they dominate other people in their environment. They like to argue and debate anything, especially if they think they can win, and especially in front of other students, so they can show dominance.

Reversing the Problem

The three legged stool. A symbol for the main philosophy for reversal is the three legged stool. It demonstrates that any treatment of the problem must involve a united front involving three persons: parents, student and a teacher or representative of the school (counselor, coach, or anyone who has an interest in the student's achievement). The stool symbolizes the belief that without one of the legs, the stool will fall down. This is also called the trifocal approach.

a. A very important aspect of this approach is that teachers should support the parents, and the parents should support the teachers, principal, coach, or whomever is the school representative.

b. Crucial to reversal is the concept of holding the student accountable. It involves success charts and progress reports and so forth as evidence of performance. Create a chart that contains: A table for missing homework, a line for evaluating behavior, a place for a teacher's signature and one for a parent's signature, and a place for a current grade. Students should also sign or initial the form.

With the student's input, decide on a point system for having no missing work and what grade is to be acceptable.

Don't try to solve all of the problems in the first step, break it down into smaller accomplishments that the student can achieve without feeling overwhelmed,

Accomplishments occur in a hierarchy beginning with appropriate behavior, putting forth effort in work completion, and finally in quality of work. (See AppendixII)

Setting goals and expectations in contracts can be done on a daily or weekly basis, depending on how severe the problem is and how often parents would like to have an update.

Another recommendation is to create a **contract** with the student's help, which contains information about the goals you agreed upon. That way there is no disagreement or confusion about what the requirements are and what the points mean, as well as the rewards when the goal is reached.

One item you may want to include in your point system and contract is that the student should **willingly** go to his study area without argument, at the appointed time, and for the entire agreed upon time.

Homework Guidelines

c. Have consistent homework rules and time, with a recommended minimum of 60 minutes for grade school, 1 and 1/2 hours for middle school and junior high, and 120 minutes for high school. Sunday through Thursday nights are school homework nights. If the student has no homework or homework does not require the allotted time, students should use the entire time for some educational activity, such as reading an age appropriate book or magazine article. Comic books, graphic novels, and most sports or teen magazines usually do not qualify as educational. They could write a thank you note or journal, read or write a poem, do a crossword puzzle, or any other creative activity. It might even be a good idea to keep a book of crossword puzzles in the house for occasions when the student needs an activity. Still another activity would be to read a newspaper while looking for typos, spelling or grammar errors. It is disappointing to find how many there can sometimes be.

No music, TV, computer or telephone distractions during homework time.

Choose some kind of reward if the student reaches a certain number of points agreed upon by all parties. Be sure the student has input in this decision. The reward should not be expensive or large, something like time with friends, time for computer games, use of driving privileges, time allowed for using a recreational electronic item, choice of a favorite meal, going to or renting a movie, privilege of or time allowed for using the car, etc.

Since underachievers have problems connecting effort with results, they often cannot connect the effort with the reward. Consequently, the reward should follow behavior promptly.

Responsibility for having the teacher fill out the form should rest with the student and should be any time that is convenient for the teacher.

Parents should require this form to be returned to them on a regular basis, perhaps one agreed upon with the teacher's input, i.e. every Friday. This responsibility might even be included as a part of the point system;

The teacher may want to have the student return the form with the parent's signature one day after it is taken home.

d. Encourage parents to establish a regular study area. Students should have a designated study area that is free from distractions, requires sitting up, and is used only for study.

The bed is not an acceptable choice, as that is reserved for sleeping or relaxation, and reclining is not conducive to producing quality homework. Students need to be upright and alert for optimum learning.

Music or, obviously TV, is also not a good idea as it takes their attention away from the task they need to accomplish.

If the student insists that they do better work with music playing, an appropriate response might be, "Your past performance has not shown this to be true," or, "When you exhibit this behavior and change the result, I'll be glad to reconsider that privilege."

e. Teacher contribution includes making a commitment to help. State and reaffirm your commitment frequently.

For dominant children, identify the strength which the student values most. Establish yourself as in control but liking the student. Arrange a brief personal and confidential meeting. Set short-term goals together and specify positive and negative consequences. Write a contractual agreement.

A dominant student will try to take control in your class. Avoid writing student's name on the board. Small daily rewards or privileges may be effective. Try reprimands, personal signals, and brief time-outs. Withdrawal of privileges are effective consequences as is withdrawal of attention. These can be added to the form used for incomplete work. Unsatisfactory days should be followed with consistent negative consequences in the contractual agreement. Be sure to work with parents on the contractual agreement.

f. Parents are encouraged to do the following to encourage an achieving attitude. Present yourself as authentic. Listen to all parties. Give information in a general way rather then accusing or diagnosing. Model positive attitudes, especially about your jobs. Emphasize the benefits of hard work and enjoyment of the job, the importance of a good paycheck, and how your performance contributes to it. Model good communication by responding to one other in a positive, supportive way, by listening to each other, and using feedback (restating statements to insure and convey understanding).

Avoid "adultizing" kids, talking to kids about things they are not ready to understand, like money issues and debt, marital problems and disagreements, balancing the family budget. At school those tasks might be grading papers, recording grades, calculating GPAs, etc.

Don't give them responsibility they are not ready to handle, like taking a family member to a doctor's appointment or taking care of an aging, ill, handicapped, or ailing family member, unless, of course, they are mature enough to handle the job. Do not permit them to enforce discipline/consequences with younger siblings.

Discuss, the negatives, but not in front of the kids.

Teachers should respect confidentiality, do not share anything about the student; set limits, limits are safety zones.

g. Both teacher and parents should set limits. Be sure that your statement is enforceable. Instead of, "Don't talk to me in that tone of voice! (nothing to enforce there), a better way of saying it is, "I'll be glad to listen when your voice is as soft as mine." Instead of saying, "Get to work on your studying," try "You are welcome to join us when your work is finished. Good luck."

Know how you plan to enforce the limit before stating it.

Avoid, "fighting words," such as telling the child what to do, like "You get to work right now!" or telling the child what you will not allow.

Avoid arguments. If a student tries to argue, remove the debate from the classroom by saying something like, "I'd be interested in hearing your idea. Could we meet after class?" Or, "I'd be interested in hearing your idea, please describe it to me." Then respond, "Let me think about it; I'll get back to you." Another option might be, "Let's try it part my way and part your way."

Listen respectfully and attentively. Take time to consider their idea. You may need to say, "Let me think about it. I will get back to you in _____. You may want to visit the teacher's lounge for thinking time and shelter. Students will value your encouragement of their ideas.

Dr. Sylvia Rimm, based on her experiences at her family achievement clinic in Wisconsin has identified twelve laws/beliefs about achievement.

Law 1: Children are more likely to be achievers if their parents join together to give the same clear and positive message about school effort and expectations.

Law 2: Children can learn appropriate behaviors more easily if they have effective models to imitate.

Law 3: What adults say to each other about a child within in his or her hearing dramatically affects that child's behaviors and self perceptions.

Law 4: If parents overreact to their children's successes and failures, the children are likely to find either intense pressure to succeed or despair and discouragement in dealing with failure.

Law 5: Children feel more tension when they are worrying about their work than when they are doing that work.

Law 6: Children develop self confidence through struggle.

Law 7: Deprivation and excess frequently exhibit the same symptoms.

Law 8: Children development confidence and an internal sense of control if they are given the power, in gradually increasing increments as they show maturity and responsibility

Law 9: Children become oppositional if one adult allies with them against a parent or a teacher, making them more powerful than the adult.

Law 10: Adults should avoid confrontations with children unless they are reasonably sure they can control the outcome.

Law 11: Children will become achievers only if they learn to function in competition.

Law 12: Children will continue to achieve if they see the relationship between the learning process and its outcomes.

Notes

CHAPTER 4: LOVE AND LOGIC LESSONS
Disciplining with dignity for both you and your students

Effective Classroom Management

I was not an authoritative teacher, so a strict black and white approach to dealing with students did not fit my style; however, clear rules and direction about consequences worked well with me. The best compliment I ever received came from a current student responding to a new student's inquiry about "Mrs. Skoog". The current student responded by saying, "She's strict but fair."

Again for me, this topic held a two-fold interest. First, I wanted to effectively manage my classroom. Second, my own children were young and I was not confident that I was handling them in the best way possible. I felt I was telling them "No" too often. I was aware of other discipline approaches, but was not comfortable with them. I felt there had to be some better ideas available somewhere. When my first school offered a class called "The Psychology of Discipline", I registered for the class immediately. It was conducted by Dr. Jim Fay, educator, lecturer, author of *Discipline With Dignity: The Science of Classroom Discipline,* and founder of the Love and Logic Institute. The phrase "Love and Logic" described exactly the approach to discipline with which I would be comfortable. This approach is based on the following beliefs:

Self –Concept:

The student's self-concept is always a prime consideration. To change the behavior, we must first change the self-concept.

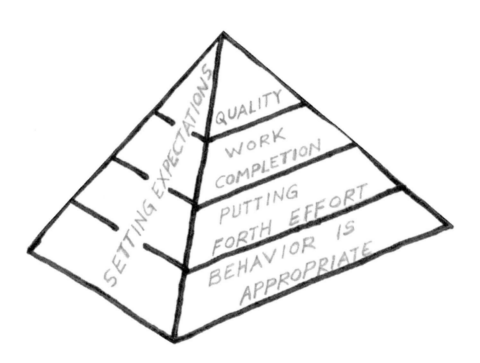

Hierarchy of Problem Solving

Control

The student is always left feeling that he has some control. Teachers learn that control is gained through investing some control in the other person. This control is offered on the adult's terms.

Consequences

An equal balance of consequences and empathy replaces punishment whenever possible. Giving kids choices and real consequences instead of punishment, and using sincere empathy with a student's problem, is based on the belief that kids now face a lot more dangerous choices then we ever faced, but have no practice in making choices for the right reasons. Dr. Fay names this Responsible Solutions.

Problem: A student forgets his book or writing utensil. Your response might be one like this . . .

"I'll bet that's very frustrating! How could you solve that problem? Would you like to know how other students have solved it? Then tell him some possible solutions.

Giving Choices

There are rules about giving them choices. Give them only choices you are willing to live with. Give only choices you can support/allow/enforce.

Make sure they understand the rule about not causing a problem for anyone else. Then if the student breaks it or argues, gently say something like, "What did I say about the first rule in problem solving?" "Does that cause a problem for anyone?" And perhaps, "Well, it does for me."

Leave the best choice for last as it may encourage him to choose the option which is preferred. Such as "I guess you could choose not to do the homework for the day and take a zero for the grade."

CHAPTER 5: MORE MATERIAL
Additional skills you can teach outside of your subject area:writing, speaking, and study skills.

Oral Presentations

See Chapter Eight.

Study Skills

Getting the most from textbooks is perhaps the most important skill you can impart to your students and it is a technique that best suits the use of your particular textbook.

- Location of Glossary and Index

- **SQ3R** study technique

  ✓ **S**urvey: Students preview the chapter noticing bold/major topic or section headings.

  ✓ **Q**uestion: Students mentally formulate a question about each heading.

  ✓ **R**ead: The next step is to read each section for details/answers to the question.

  ✓ **R**ecite: Verbalize the main content of each section.

  ✓ **R**eview: Mentally or on paper review the contents of each section.

Note Taking

Main word or symbol: Have students either use steno paper or divide notebook paper into thirds. They should be instructed to write as many details as they can in the right hand column. They should then write a main/heading word or symbol that represents the content of the notes column.

Dictating notes to the class: Speak slowly and clearly. Pause approximately every 90 seconds to allow students to catch up with the main words or symbols. It is helpful at this time to briefly review at least what you believe to be the main words for the material you have covered.

Handouts do not serve the same purpose as note taking because it is a more passive technique. Note taking requires active listening and assists in memory of the material, although they do work well as study guides if the purpose of your lecture is to review.

Additional memory devices for lectures:

- Use of acronyms

Beginning letters of the concepts you wish them to learn, assigned to a sentence about that topic. In music, one of the most common acronyms is used to help remember notes of the lines of the staff (Every Good Boy Does Fine).

In other subject areas you can just use the first letters of the concept. In social studies, the first letters of the Great Lakes form the word "HOMES" (**H**uron, **O**ntario, **M**ichigan, **E**rie & **S**uperior).

- Use of alliterations

When the first sound of each word is the same, you have alliteration. "Mountains make memorable moments." In math, "simplification makes simple solutions." "Characterization creates clear characters."

Collaborate with Other Subject Areas

One of the most interesting and rewarding projects in which I participated was a joint project with the social studies teacher about countries in Africa.

The social studies teacher assigned or allowed students to choose a country in Africa. She then required the students to research important aspects about their country such as imports, exports, geography, main cities, or flag design.

Students were asked to create a 3-D poster to show the researched information.

As the language arts teacher, I assigned an essay about that information to be followed by an oral presentation explaining their posters.

Each teacher graded their individually assigned parts including accuracy, effort and completion.

The 3-D poster appealed to both the visual and hands-on learners and was an effective and interesting way for the class to learn about many African countries. This project could also have included a fill-in-the-blank page to be filled out about each country to encourage good listening skills.

This kind of collaboration would also work well with science or even math, with some creativity.

Time Management Skills

Using Planners: Encourage students to enter workdays for assignments in their planner on the day before it is due, especially for long-term assignments. Discourage use of loose paper to avoid loss of important notes or assignments. "Sticky notes" for assignment details might be helpful. Encourage them to handle all worksheets only once. Look a worksheet over briefly when it is received, then file it in one of three places.

- To work on
- To hand in
- To throw away

Remind them to move ahead in their calendar to mark long-term assignments and "work on" dates.

Notes

CHAPTER 6: CREATING COOPERATIVE COMMUNITIES
Creative ways to form small groups with rules, activities, and assignment ideas

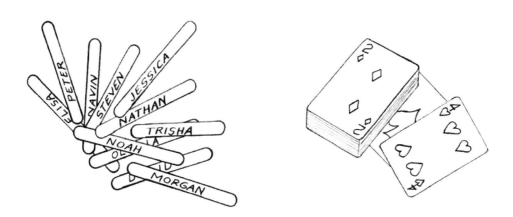

Grouping Techniques

Popsicle sticks

At the beginning of the year, or as soon as possible, acquire some craft/popsicle sticks, and write student's names on them. You could keep them in a cup on your desk and explain that they are off-limits to students.

When you are ready to use them to group students, just take them out by the handful and randomly pull the desired number of sticks for each group. You may want to have an aide or trusty student pull the sticks, or you may have one student pull a stick, then that person could pull the next stick and so forth.

Playing Cards

Before class take a deck of cards and take out the number of cards in suits equal to the number of groups you want for the activity. Then take those numbers which equal the number of students per group. If you want four groups of five students, take out cards 1-5 in each suit. Make sure you have the same number of cards as you have students in the class and then shuffle them a sufficient number of times to mix them.

As students enter the classroom, give each a card. Tell them you will explain their purpose later, and they should be careful not to lose or damage the card or swap cards with anyone.

When you are ready to begin the activity, send each group to a designated area to do the activity. You could group them either by number or suit, depending on how many groups you wish to ultimately have.

Clothing

This works particularly well if you have "spirit days" when students are permitted to wear school colors or letter jackets. The permission may depend on your dress code, school spirit colors or other ideas. You can group your students by shoe color, shirt color, those wearing jeans, or sweatshirts and so forth.

Textbook Numbers

Have students group by the last digit of their textbook number (odd or even).

Names

Divide the alphabet into smaller groups depending upon the first letters of names in your class. For example, A-G, K-M, N-Z, etc. Then, using either first or last names, have them group in this way

Rules for Small Group Activities

I acquired information for this topic from other teachers and substitues and from a workshop I attended on Cooperative Learning.

Clearly state times for everything, including getting into groups.

Give them a warning when time is almost up.

Don't be afraid to give more time if you see many are not finished with that task.

Assign or have groups choose students for different roles as needed for the activity i.e.

- Chairman/facilitator (leader) is responsible for guiding the group to stay on the activity/task, completing all the activity. Including all group members making sure all aspects of the activity are finished according to directions.

- Secretary/recorder, etc.

- Presenter, etc.

- Explain the job/responsibilities for each role. Remind all students that this is a group activity and all are expected to participate.

Don't feel as if you need to have each group complete all of the activity. You could divide it among the groups

Circulate among the groups to check on/encourage equal participation and to insure that all are included. For example, if you have a worksheet or section for the activity with 20 questions and examples, and you have five groups, give each group four of the problems. Then each group "teaches" their answers to the rest of the class, including how they arrived at that answer at the end of the activity.

To grade the group participants fairly, I would ask the secretary/recorder to make sure names of all those who participated in the activity are on the sheet before handing it in. You can then record grades for all equally.

Another activity that works well in small groups is the arranging of a sentence, quote, or definition, and example of a concept. Put each part of the item you wish them to put together on an index card, and give each group a stack of cards, briefly explaining what they are to accomplish.

You could make it a competition so that the first group to correctly finish will win a prize.

Projects Outside of School

I would discourage the use of projects outside of school unless you have an area of the topic that cannot be covered as an in-class project. Then you may wish to implement these suggestions:

- Give student's time to exchange phone numbers so they can contact each other to arrange work times.

- Encourage the group to divide the project into separate tasks with due dates assigned to keep the project on track for the final due date. A group should give you a copy of the assignments. This also allows you the ability to assign grades individually.

Large Group Activities

Rules: All the rules are the same as for small group activities, but it is especially important here to give time limits to discourage socialization.

Roles: Assign or ask for volunteers for the different roles, except, of course, you are the leader/facilitator.

Types of Activities

1. **Bingo** – You can create Bingo cards in a variety of ways. These are often good ways to review concepts before a test, and they do not require grading.☺

For grammar parts of speech, the cards could be made with 4 columns and 4-5 rows and filled in with words of random parts of speech. You could head the columns

W.O.R.D., then during the game you would "call" things like, "under W, find a noun," under R, find a verb," etc. The first person with four in a row wins. (The prize could be any one of a number of things).

I tried to keep bite size candy bars hidden in my room for such occasions; however, if I had nothing available, I often told them I'd bring them a can of soda the next day, or offer "free homework coupon"

You could put random words on the card and head the columns **NOUN, VERB, PRON, ADJ, PREP,** or whichever part of speech you are studying at the time. Copy enough of these to have one for each student. Then when you hand them out tell the students to find all words that fit the part of speech under the heading, the first to find four in a row wins.

When the student calls out the words to be approved as a legitimate bingo, and you determine that they are valid, you have a ready grade when they turn in their "card" with their name on it.

Sentence Formation Structure

This is a good active, hands-on learning experience, a rare occurrence in a Language Arts Class. To begin, formulate a sentence. Write each word of the sentence on a different piece of construction paper or art paper, writing the word on both sides of the paper large enough to be seen from across the room. You may want to laminate these, depending on the age and personalities of your class.

Hand out the papers randomly.

Ask two students with noun words to come forward and one student with a verb. Continue with this until you have called to the front all parts of speech you have used in the sentence. This gives the students a review of the parts of speech. Have them meet off to the side of the room to decide what the sentence is supposed to say. If you are studyingliterature, you could use a quote from the piece. In math or science, you could use a definition or example of a concept, in history, create a description or event from a particular time period.

Have them stand across the front of the room, holding the paper so the rest of the class can see the word. Since the word is also on the back, the student can see the word he is holding for the rest of the activity.

If you are studying sentence structure, ask the students who are standing with the cards to separate the sentence between the subject and the verb. If there are any prepositional phrases, ask them to move to one side of the rest of the sentence, since neither the subject nor the verb can occur in a prepositional phrase. Point this out to the students as a further review if you are studying sentence diagramming.

Barrel of Monkeys

I adapted this idea from a local radio station which used it for listeners to request or suggest a song by title. For the classroom, you could

a. Give them a topic/category to work with.

b. The object/rule is for each student to give an item/example that fits the topic in the category, but it must begin with the last letter of the previous one given previously, etc. Activity ends when no one can give a word that fits the requirements, when time runs out or when all students have had the opportunity to participate.

In a Language Arts class, the topics could be a part of speech in grammar, a list of characters or details about the setting. In Math or Science, it might be an example or characteristic of the concept being studied. In history, it might be an example or characteristic of the time or area being studied.

Example: If you are asking the class for examples of nouns you don't need to but you could start at the beginning of the alphabet, the first student might say, "ant," since it ends in "t" the next word should begin with a "t". If the next person says, "tea" the third student would need to think of a noun that begins with "a", for example, "apple", now the fourth person might say "elephant". This would continue until the students can no longer think of an appropriate word or until all students have participated in the exercise. If students are having difficulty following the rules you may need to guide them by saying, "Okay the next word needs to begin with ____". You might at any time switch the category to any word or adjectives.

CHAPTER 7: CLASSROOM AIDES
Using help as efficiently as possible

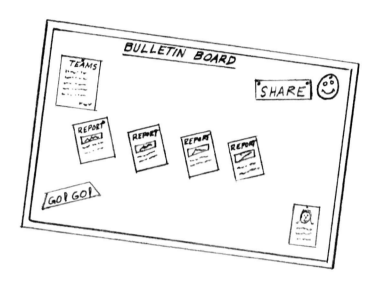

Non Academic Help

Bulletin boards: Assign the aide the task of designing a theme. Make sure the aide submits the idea to you for approval before beginning construction.

Encourage the use of color and figurative language which is effective in getting students' attention and helping to make it memorable. Be careful not to use answers to future tests, especially spelling words.

Use of appropriate symbols also impacts effectiveness of the bulletin board, especially holiday symbols, as those help create a festive atmosphere in the classroom which encourages students to feel a holiday mood which, believe it or not, usually results in fewer behavior problems and management issues.

Lamination Jobs: Laminating is important because it insures longevity of your design, enabling you to use it again or utilize parts of it in future themes.

An aide could do the laminating for you or the aide could simply cut out what you have laminated.

Laminating prevents pieces from falling or being rubbed off by students, or tearing simply from use.

Passes: The aide could fill out hall passes or referrals to the office, counselor, or the library as long as they clearly understand your classroom rules about issuing passes.

Miscellaneous Classroom Contributions

The aide could be in charge of decorating the classroom for holidays, can distribute prizes to winners of small group competitions or other academic contests, and may even be willing to do the purchasing of the prizes.

The aide could design answer sheets for tests or quizzes. Simply give the aide the test and ask them to design an answer sheet that would be easy to use for grading.

Copying answer sheets, worksheets or tests is another task the aide can perform.

If asking the aide to grade papers, you may want to design your own easy answer sheets.

Blanks down the left side of the answer sheet for multiple choice or true/false questions are helpful.

Instead of essay questions, it is better to use "outline" or "lists" questions as these are less subjective and easier for the aide to evaluate.

Checklists for completion are another idea for grading work.

If grading is a task you would like the aide to perform, paper clip a copy of your key on top of each class' papers with point values printed for each question or section. Make sure it is clear whether you are grading by percentages or points, and whether you would like the aide to mark the number wrong, or the number right.

It is true that the easy answer sheets would be simple for you to grade, but you will have an adequate amount of work without grading as well.

Help in Academic Areas

Some schools have specific rules about what non teachers (aides) are allowed to do with students assignments or tests as far as grading goes, for privacy issues. For the same reason, recording grades in your grade book may be a problem. If it is allowed, this is a good use of the aide's time. Be sure to explain to the aide your policy or procedure for recording grades so that what the Aid does is consistent with your entries.

Finding Aides

Some schools may have a volunteer coordinator. If you tell that person specifically what kind of aides you are looking for and the amount of time you wish the aide to work, that coordinator can probably find an appropriate volunteer for your needs.

Student aids can be just as helpful. Some schools may even offer credit for students who help in a classroom.

Often Honor Societies or other organizations will require members to perform some type of service; so approaching that group's sponsor with your need could result in help for your classroom.

Often there are senior citizens or retired teachers who would like to be involved in the school.

With any aide it is advisable to hold an orientation meeting. Discuss your technique for grading, recorded grades, and any other tasks you may ask them to perform.

CHAPTER 8: ORAL PRESENTATIONS
Easy delivery techniques you can teach your students for class and for "real life situations"

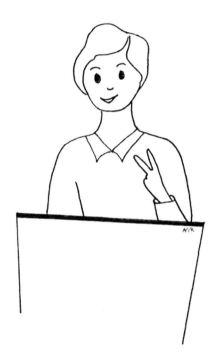

Do not leave teaching oral presentations skills to the speech or English teacher, as oral presentations can greatly enhance the learning process - especially if students are encouraged to "teach" a concept or a section. Teaching the rest of the class can help the presenter learn and remember the information better. If you assign posters, dioramas, or other projects you might require students to present and explain their projects to the class. This is especially effective if the project is made about a country or a concept being studied.

Dramas and puppet shows can be used in classes other than language arts to teach a concept or present information to the class in an interesting format. Students often are more receptive to drama presentations and more willing to participate in this kind of project because they can present as a different persona.

Delivery Techniques

These are easier to teach than you might imagine.

✓ Posture

Discourage the "fig leaf" stance. Instead, encourage students to use their hands for gesturing and quietly holding their notes. Call to their attention that speakers often have unconscious habits that surface when they are nervous such as putting their hands in their pockets, playing with their hair, and so forth. Also, discourage the stiff military stance, which contributes to "wobbling". It can also result in fainting if the student "locks knees" which cuts off circulation to the brain.

The best and most comfortable posture is the "T" formation of the feet, slightly separated. This results in a more balanced posture, which prevents "wobbling," or fainting, and allows the student to concentrate on the speech instead of worrying about posture.

✓ **Voice**

This may seem like it should be automatic, but most people do not think about it. To begin with, students should know that most people tend to speed up when speaking in front of an audience.

Practicing with a timer will help prevent this as the speaker can get a feel for the proper pace.

If students are given a time limit, this will also give them a goal to work toward. A time limit should include a minimum and a maximum time and you should deduct points if the student speaks over or under the limits. You may wish to implement a grace period, perhaps of thirty seconds.

It is also helpful for the speaker if their speech is divided into a time limit for each part. For example, the introduction should be approximately thirty seconds in a three to five minute speech. The body of the speech will be approximately one and one half minutes. The conclusion will also last approximately thirty seconds.

✓ **Eye Contact and Facial Expression**

Have eye contact with all areas of the audience, and avoid the "ping-pong" effect. Let your face show interest and enthusiasm for your topic.

✓ **Movement**

Should be deliberate and purposeful, used only to emphasize main point or transition to the next point.

✓ **Gestures**

Should be natural, not forced. Avoid overly planned-looking gestures like the "quote" gesture using two fingers of both hands.

✓ **Visual Aids**

Obviously visual aid should large enough to be seen in the back of the classroom. Encourage the use of color, but students should avoid light or bright colors that are distracting and difficult to read. Fancy "fonts" or shadowing is also hard to read.

Discourage students from bringing items to be passed around as a visual aid.

If students have the capability, power point presentations are always an effective attention-getting way of adding visual aids to their presentation. Caution students about use of like color letters on the same colored background or reverse colors of light colors on dark backgrounds. Some graphics are also difficult to see clearly.

CHAPTER 9: VAT TEACHING
Teaching to different learning styles
(Visual, Auditory, and Tactile Learners)

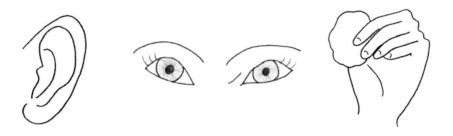

One of my strengths was my creative ability to find different styles and techniques of teaching to types of projects. Consequently, teaching to different learning styles for me only required polishing and refining. This was accomplished adequately by attending a class in "4-Mat Learning Styles." Through this I learned not only how to identify the learning styles, but also how to design units that would include all of the learning styles. It is not necessary to include all styles every day, but throughout a lesson. With my enjoyment of different teaching styles and projects, I eagerly looked for ways to reach each style.

Visual Learners

This category is the most common type of learner, and the easiest to work with. These students respond well to use of color on the board or in handouts, and use of graphics and symbols.

It is important to write assignments on the board in addition to saying them out loud. They also easily gain information from slide presentations or videos.

Auditory Learners

These are the learners most commonly reached, since teachers like to talk and lecture.

Be sure to say assignments and due dates clearly.

Recorded stories or spelling words, are effective for these learners. Books on tape or CDs are great for these students as well.

You may want to record explanations or concepts for learners who show strong tendencies for this learning style.

Be sure to read directions aloud, as this will also benefit other learners.

Include in project options those activities that would be heard, for example, puppet shows, skits, oral presentations, and "teaching" the class from worksheets or concepts.

Ask all students to read aloud from the textbook.

Have them read sentence by sentence instead of an entire section.

Allow them to skip words they cannot pronounce. You could fill in those words, but it is not helpful to allow other students to do this.

When reading drama it is not necessary to assign parts, simply ask the next person to read the next part. Students will still understand the meaning.

If reading short stories, a project which would also involve writing might be to ask students to create a "play" from the story. You might even ask them to choose actors for the parts, and a theme song which would fit the story. Remind them to include directions for movement.

Tactile Learners

These students are the most difficult to teach because most subject areas are not naturally hands-on, with the exception of science.

In language arts, I would write words of a sentence to teach sentence structure or use a quotation from literature. I would write the words on construction paper, front and back, and laminate them for longevity. I would hand out the "cards" randomly to students either in small groups or the entire class.

For sentence structure, I would call students with words of a particular part of speech to the front of the classroom and ask them to stand in the order that would create a complete sentence. Then depending on what was being studied, I would have certain parts of speech sit down. If we were studying prepositions I would ask the prepositions student to sit down, then I would ask the rest of the class if the sentence was still accurate.

If we were studying diagramming, I would ask the students who were part of a prepositional phrase to sit down, since neither the subject nor predicate can be found in a prepositional phrase. Then I would ask the students to separate between the subject and the verb/predicate. And again, I would ask the remainder of the class if that was correct. If they believed it was wrong, I would require them to explain why and what would be correct.

When using quotes from literature I would ask students to decide among the group the order of the words to form a correct quote. Then I would ask them to take or somehow place the words in the correct order on the board after standing at the front of the classroom. Then I would ask the rest of the class for the name of the speaker and situation where the quote occurred.

In other subject areas, cards could contain examples or definitions of a concept or area time period being studied.

Projects should also include some options that would involve hands-on production.

Building models, dioramas, and 3-D posters using food items or styrofoam pieces for concepts such as molecules, solar system, land formations, continents, or scenes.

Another project I have used was making costumes, either for themselves or for dolls or simply freestanding. These could be created from fabric or paper and will involve some research.

To further expand this project into other areas, students might give an oral presentation explaining their designs, or write an essay for the same purpose.

Identifying Learning Styles

There is a "Learning Style Index" available for classroom use. Your counselor or special education teacher may have access to this. Other suggestions include the following.

You can, in individual conferences, ask questions of students to establish their learning style. You can check with previous teachers.

Notes

CHAPTER 10: HANDLING THE PAPER LOAD
Alternatives to detailed grading when faced with that mountain of papers you need to grade

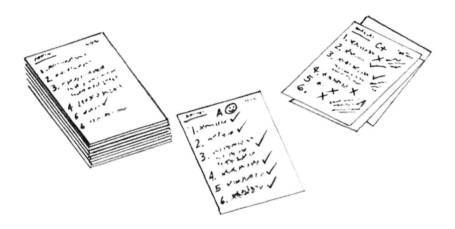

Packets

Instead of grading each worksheet or assignment separately, it often is effective to combine those into a packet for a chapter/unit.

At the beginning of the chapter/unit hand out a list of items you want them to include and requirements for each item as well as the entire packet.

     a. Neatness
     b. Completeness
     c. Following directions

d. Effort and anything else you have as goals for the project.

Packets could include handout/worksheets, as well as assignments from the textbook, or examples of concepts.

As a language arts teacher, I used a packet of the entire concept of poetry asking for examples of each type of poetry or figurative language. You can also ask for drawings or charts.

Checklists

Instead of grading for individual points of an assignment, many times you need only grade for completed items. Packets is one example.

Weekly, chapter/unit assignments could all be listed on one checklist.

If you prefer to check on the due date for each assignment, you would just carry your checklist around the room and check off those students who could show you a completed assignment.

Students could then put the assignment in a packet that you could collect later.

On your checklist, especially for your packet, you could include things for quality, such as neatness, following directions, effort, and meeting due dates promptly.

Techniques for Grading Writing Assignments

Grade for a single skill with each paper instead of grading for everything with each one.

Grade one paper for organization. Grade for punctuation according to the one you are studying at the time, apostrophe, semi-colon, parenthesis, etc. Another paper could be graded for capital letters, or complete sentences.

Six-Trait Writing Skills

I learned a different method of teaching and evaluating written assignments.

a. Voice: Students' ability to use words and phrases so that the paper sounds individual rather than like everyone else's.

b. Word choice: This includes using the right word as well as creative word choices.

c. Organization: This includes topic sentences and supporting details for smaller writings and introductory paragraphs, body paragraphs, conclusions, and using transitions between each part.

d. Fluency: This refers to use of complete sentences throughout, transition words between sentences, and use of commas with introductory phrases.

e. Mechanics: This refers to all punctuation and spelling issues, as well as typos.

f. Sentence structure: This trait is evaluated on completeness, as well as agreement between subject and verb and noun/pronoun.

You would teach one trait at a time but grade for all traits with a paper.

Each trait is graded on a scale of one to five, five being the best.

You might create a small graph of six squares, one for each trait. As you read through the paper, you only need get a general idea about the quality of each trait and write down a number value.

If you prefer to use percentages, simply convert the 30 point system to percentages.

CHAPTER 11: OCCUPYING OPENERS
Techniques for starting a class that will allow you to complete those tasks which are necessary for beginning the class

"Mod minutes" (Modification Examples)

Write a sentence or problem on the board with at least one error. Give students a time limit; one to two minutes is usually adequate.

Have students write the corrected version of the sentence/problem in a "journal" or notebook which they use strictly for your class.

Of course you would have needed to add this to the list of required materials to bring to each class.

This could be graded using a checklist for accuracy or simply for having the correct number of entries.

SSR (Sustained Silent Reading)

Ask the students to bring reading material of your limitations to each class. Give them sixty seconds in which to read their material silently.

This could also be used for a time when they may review for a test.

To encourage responsibility and checking on participation in the activity, you could have them also write in the journal or notebook a summary of the contents of their reading or review.

This would be graded using a checklist only for having an entry for each day of the grading period you have chosen.

You might choose to only grade this at the end of the quarter or weekly.

I usually required the students to write the date at the top of each entry to facilitate easy grading.

The date was part of the points that were given,. No date resulted in a deduction of one point per entry.

Journal/Log

Write a topic or important term on the board (establish a time limit) and ask the students to write their thoughts on the topic, or a definition or sentence for the word or the term given in their journal.

If you are trying to encourage complete sentences, you may want to require a certain number of complete sentences for the entry.

If their assignment was reading you could ask them to write a summary of the material or key points from the assignment as their journal entry. You could also ask them to write the page numbers read.

Notes

CHAPTER 12: CONFIDENCE THROUGH COMPETITION
Helping students find their comfort zone

As Dr. Rimm states in "Miles of Achievement," "Children will become achievers only if they learn to function in competition."

Dr. Rimm has found that many students drop out of college because they never learned to function in a competitive environment. She recommends encouraging achievement by including a variety of competitive activities in your teaching techniques. These include the following:

- ✓ Competition between groups
- ✓ Between individuals within a group.
- ✓ Competition within themselves.

Some examples of effective competition that she mentioned are included in the following paragraphs.

Four H Club projects are a fine way to experience competition. I can echo that wisdom because I had ten years of Four H projects from which to learn: I experienced more due to competitive aspect of exhibiting at the county or state fairs or other exhibitions than I did in simply completing the project with the directions given in the project book. In the project books I learned the basic "How-To". In competition, I learned to do the project *better*. This competition was with others with the goal to earn a first place ribbon as well as with myself to earn a better individual ribbon than the previous year. My experience was both in product/projects, as well as with performance areas such as demonstrations and group musical performances. The latter I learned from previous year's performances and from watching other group's performances. I learned what it took to earn the top ribbons, including topics and techniques. This experience, then, taught me what to do with my own projects and performances to improve my skills. In my case, the projects were displayed for examination by visitors to the exhibit building as well as by other exhibitors. In this way we each could see for ourselves the difference between characteristics of the different award levels for the projects. From this information I learned how I should change my project for the next year to earn higher awards. In the case of performance competitions, critical information resulted from comparing ourselves to other competitors as well as written critiques of our own performances. There were similar comparisons/critiques for the projects. In this way my competition came from both other competitors and within myself. The times I learned perhaps the most ways to improve were when I worked as a judge's assistant and could both see the projects and hear the judge's comments. So, it was clear how I could improve.   This competition resulted in an increase in self-esteem which lasted throughout my lifetime, in both performing and producing items for myself or my family. As a result, I was able to sing in various performing groups as well as in solo situations. I was able to create clothing for my family, as well as making the gowns for my own wedding.

Another competition which had a great impact on my self-esteem was music competition. Our school district participated in regional competitions. I competed both as a solo performer and as a member of several performance groups. In this kind of competition, judges were allowed to give oral critiques at the end of each performance. In this way I learned how to improve for the next performance. My performances were not always successes, but I learned perhaps even more from my failures. I learned how to improve: however, even the failures increased my self-esteem because I learned how to deal handle failures without falling apart. I learned that I could improve in spite of the disappointment of not doing as well as I had hoped.

The next example of effective competition I experienced was as a coach rather a participant. This activity was forensics (competitive speech and debates.) Forensics is entirely an individual competition, but the individual gains experience and esteem that will transfer into group settings. This competition relies on written critiques and watching fellow students. Competitors can still use both methods to improve their own performances for the next tournament even though they are not allowed to see critique sheets during a tournament. They can improve their performance for the next round of competition by comparing themselves to other performers in their area of competition. I also found this activity to be one in which all competitors were supportive of each other and would critique each other outside of the section of their competition. I always gave critique sheets to my students after the tournament so they could improve based on their performances at that tournament. In addition to written critiques students were ranked against each other. In this way students could judge their own performance by comparing themselves to the other competitors in their events. In this area I was able to witness the growth of one student from a timid speaker to a very confident and effective valedictorian speaker. These students could also learn and gain self-esteem from their failures through these same critiques. Their confidence grew with each tournament in which they competed.

Dr. Rimm also reinforces the importance of competition in her Underachievement Newsletter, "Issue # 2", when she says, "Underachieving students have often improved their achievement with the confidence that comes from participating in a competitive group activity. Team support teaches them to cope with success and failure so they don't feel like "losers."

One final thought about competition: Children need the opportunity to fail. Mostly they need to learn how to recover from failing, and move on, maybe even achieving more than they would have before failing. Appendix II has a list of famous people who did just that. This could be used to encourage students to keep trying after failing.

CHAPTER 13: ACCOUNTABILITY
Teaching students how to be responsible and getting them to take responsibility for their choices.

Chapter Four discusses the steps of teaching responsibility and how to get students to solve their own problems, and getting students to take responsibility and face the consequences of their choices helps to counter underachievement and promote achievement. This requires holding students accountable for their actions. Help is available from the Family Achievement Clinic of Dr. Sylvia B. Rimm in Cleveland, Ohio.

Michael Cornale, an associate with Dr. Rimm's Family Achievement Clinic, identifies some recommendations for effective accountability. The first is "Accountability should not be delayed if possible, since accountability should be regular and consistent (such as every Friday) because it will be more effective for achievement. Students are more likely to achieve if they see the relationship between effort and result. This only happens if there is not too much delay in feedback.

The second characteristic of effective accountability is that it should be short term, for the same reason, covering one day or one week as opposed to an entire grading period (quarter, semester). A sample of an evaluation form is included at the end of this chapter in the Appendix.

The third characteristic is that it involves ongoing home life and school communication. A periodical evaluation form to be signed by both parent and teacher is effective.

The fourth characteristic is that you should reduce the sensation of the response to the accountability. In other words, eliminate high magnitude responses and negative responses to the issue of accountability. Cornale and Dr. Rimm suggest using some of the following anti arguing instructions, since dominant students pride themselves on their debating skills and know that you are more vulnerable if they argue in front of the class. If they lose in front of their peers, they inspire peer sympathy. If they win, peer admiration. If you lose in front of the class, you lose respect from the students. If you win, they side with the "poor student." Therefore, when the arguer raises his/her hand, "I've got a better way to do this math," immediately remove the debate from the classroom arena by a positive response like, "I'd be very interested in hearing about your idea, let's meet right after class."

After class, don't say yes or no to the student. Instead say, "Please describe your idea." Or "Could you tell me what you have in mind?"

If you are not sure how you want to respond when interrupted in class, say, "Let me think about it; I'll get back to you."

It isn't necessary to convince the student that you are right, only to hear him/her out, and to be willing to make reasonably flexible compromises. You must positively trust that the student will honor the commitment he/she has made. Your goal is to stay in a positive alliance with the student with such logical statements as, "I like the way you think." Or "I trust you will keep your word, you are fair and honest. I know I can count on you." (S. Rimm, Learning Leads Que Cards, Apple Publishing Company, Watertown, WI. 1990.)

The purpose of the anti-arguing technique is to avoid being angry. It is believed that when adults respond to a student's behavior, the student will concentrate on the anger and not see the consequences.

The final characteristic is that quality of work should reflect positive regard for the accountability process, perhaps commenting something like, "I appreciate your attention to completing your evaluation form," or, "I'm glad to see you're doing so well."

When using a periodic evaluation it is important that the student be responsible for acquiring the teacher's help in filling out the form. This would involve approaching the teacher about an appropriate time to ask for his or her assistance, one that would not be an inconvenience for him or her, as well as doing the same for his parents. As the teacher you may wish to require parents' signatures on the evaluation form to insure that they have read the form. You may even ask the student to sign it before sending it home to show that he agrees and understands the comments.

The design of the evaluation form, if different from the sample given, should be a collaboration between teacher and parent to effect the kind of information that parents wish to receive, as well as the information that will be most helpful for the student's achievement. This might include noting the missing assignments, comments on behavior, current grade and quality of homework. It might also change with the student's improvement.

Another factor which influences students' success in school is the effect of outside influences, especially the many kinds of available technological advances. These includ cell phones, hand held data instruments, and mp3 players. The latter is especially problematic because it is small enough to be easily hidden. These devices are not only invasive distractions to listening to the teacher's instructions, but also interfere with the student's time for completing classroom work. Additionally, it has not been proven, but the types of music listened to and the games played may have a negative impact on the student's behavior in class as well as outside of school. Another disruptive activity, comparable to old school-style notes passed between students is the ability to send text messages between students. These not only disrupt the student writing the message, but also the recipient. Some students may argue that they can "text" so rapidly that it isn't really a distraction, but any process which occupies a student's concentration or thought process interferes with the learning process. It also raises potential problems with cheating on tests. Pagers are another potential for disruption as they are noisier than other devices. Additionally, some students have been known to use them for illegal activities. Parents may insist on the student having that kind of immediate availability, but you may suggest that the students only be allowed to use them during lunch hour or class breaks and recommend that parents have a copy of their student's schedule so this can be accomplished. If these become a recurring problem you may want to talk to your administrator and request school rules about using such items during school time or even having them in possession. Some schools have even confiscated the items if a student is caught with them. You can probably always include them in your own classroom rules. You may want to consult with your administrator about acceptable procedures for establishing your rules. Many administrators may only require a list of your rules so that they are aware of them for potential communication with parents. There may also be legal issues of which you are not aware.

In addition to technological devices, other outside influences include fellow students, perhaps from a different school. This may happen at extra curricular activities, such as scholastic, sports and other competitions. Negative influences can be affected by strong supervision or at least visible representation of the faculty at these events. Although this may require additional use of your time, it serves two purposes: not only does it limit possible negative influences by other students; it also shows your students that you care about their lives outside the classroom.

In addition, students are obviously affected by their home situation, whether it is separated parents, a seriously ill parent, or additional family members who live in the home. All can impact a student's performance.

Negative impact might be decreased by techniques such as recommending that the student check out a second text book to keep with the non-custodial parent in the case of a split custody situation. Another way that is often helpful is to meet with the student's other teachers so that all are aware of the situation and can share techniques they have found to be effective. It would be a good idea to include the parent (s) in this meeting to get their preferences and input on any solutions. Including a counselor may also be helpful.

Believe it or not, other teachers can also have an impact on student achievement or behavior in your class. If they have different or conflicting roles, it may be necessary to remind students that the rules in other classrooms do not affect the rules in your classroom. Rules for your classroom are to be observed any time a student is in your room, be that during class time or when coming to you for extra help. If students are confused by this you might want to suggest they keep a copy of each class' rules in their text books. It may be helpful to review your rules periodically, for example, at the beginning of each quarter.

To insure parents support of my rules I always required a parent's signature on a copy of the rules at the beginning of the year, I even sometimes offered a few extra credit points for a prompt return of the signed document.

In all classrooms, it is advisable to at least be aware of the possible outside influences and be prepared to deal with them. Simply communicating to students that you are aware of the existence of these negative influences will sometimes be enough to discourage their use or eliminate a problem with them. A promise to notify parents of the issue will also deter their use.

On the other side, the use of a personal data assistant might be encouraged for use as a planner for homework, due dates and requirements. However it should be reinforced that using a PDA should not occur during the time you are conducting class, or the time students are to be completing classroom work. Your preference about using the planner may influence this practice. Above all, it is important not to penalize those students who do not have access such devices.

Notes

CHAPTER 14: FINAL TIPS

Banking

TIP: Use banking as a learning tool in your class

TECHNIQUE
- The items you have that students may want to borrow are your "merchandise"
- You set the price/collateral required etc.

Here are some ideas
- One item donated to the treasure chest, one like item to be returned when the borrowed item is returned
- One Privilege Coupon
- You are the main bank, the rest of the students are branch banks, and can loan items as well. They determine the price of their "merchandise"
- When a student wishes to borrow something from any "bank," he must "pay" for it before it becomes his possession
- You might even create a receipt similar to the sample below

GUIDELINES:
- Do not take/ask for driver's licenses as payment/collateral, for obvious reasons

- If student does not keep his end of a deal or return it by the required time, it or the payment will be repossessed (i.e. confiscated)
- It would be advisable to write a copy of your policy on this practice at the beginning of the year, and maybe even ask for a parent's signature to be sure everyone understands the practice.
- If a student wishes to purchase an item instead of borrowing, he forfeits his payment to the seller
- If the student is taking out a loan on the item, collateral will be returned upon return of the borrowed item, if returned by the due date. If it is not, he either forfeits his collateral or is fined/charged a "fee" determined in advance by the lender.

Benefits:
- Students get a "real life" learning experience
- More than just in your subject area, you give them a life-skill

Sample Receipt on following page.

LOAN DOCUMENT/SALES RECEIPT

Name_____ **Date**_____

Item borrowed _____

Return date_____

LOAN   PURCHASE (circle one)

Payment / Collateral _____

Item return date _____

Games

TIP: Using games in your class has two benefits: (1) It serves to bring a higher level of fun (something uncommon in the school classroom.) and (2) it often gets students up and moving, which helps them stay alert

TECHNIQUE -
1. Adapt an existing board game to your classroom.
2. To create "spaces" (such as would be found on a board game) use construction paper placed or taped around the room perimeter, as well as through the aisles. If necessary, mark some with geometric shapes to differentiate them.
3. Using index cards, create card sets as needed by the game. For example:
   a. Create question cards, using questions or problems from a current unit of study or review for upcoming test. It might be helpful to number these and keep a corresponding number page of answers at your desk, rather than writing the answers on the back of the cards
   b. Game or movement cards like he following:
      - lose a turn
      - move ahead 3 spaces, or move to the next red/triangle space
      - Draw a question card—correct answer = draw a privilege card or move ahead ____ spaces; incorrect answer = return a

privilege card, or move back ____
spaces

   c. Privilege Cards These might include things like the following:
- Free tardy
- Free pass
- Free food/drink day
- Free or late homework (not good for major/long-term projects/papers)
- Free trip to the treasure chest or a piece of candy

4. For games requiring large dice, here is a method:
   a. Buy a piece of foam approx. 3 inches thick
   b. Cut it into cubes (an electric knife works best)
   c. From black felt cut 21 1.2-1 inch diameter "dots
   d. Glue dots to cubes like on a dice. Make a single or pair depending on your need/planned game
   e. If you need your cards to be in suits, you could either change the suits to be geometric shapes you can easily draw, or from an old deck of cards, cut the corners off and glue them to the index cards.

GUIDELINES:

1. You may want/need to have your administrator approve your Privilege Cards and/or type of game.
2. Stay away from using money, even pretend money, as part of the game. Instead, consider using Privilege Cards as your currency.
3. Write out rules/directions and give a copy to each student/team
4. If you design your own game, be sure all can participate, either individually or in teams, and that all can see the parts of the game.
5. Examples given are only ideas, use them or create your own based on your need, comfort level, class make-up and facilities
6. Avid games commonly associated with gambling, i.e. poker, blackjack, etc.

IDEAS FOR GAMES YOU CAN ADAPT:

- *Life*
- *Trivial Pursuit*
- *Jeopardy*
- *Don't Forget The Lyrics* could become, "Don't Forget The Definition (or Equation or Quote or Characteristic, etc.) Given part of the definition, student would need to finish it.

Free Late Homework Coupon

TIP: Using a Free Late Homework Coupon to reinforce a desired behavior sends a powerful message of encouragement to students that these are worth earning

TECHNIQUE:

Create a coupon similar to the sample below to award students for any number of positive behaviors

- This would allow him/her to turn in one assignment a day late without being penalized
- My exception to the privilege is that it could not be used for a presentation or other major or long-term assignment, such as a project or research paper

(sample)

FREE LATE HOMEWORK COUPON

Name _____

Assignment_____ -

Due date_____

Turned in _____ -

GRADE (_____ **)**

Good Deed Notification Forms

TIP: Notify parents when their student has done something good, these will exponentially increase your value in the eyes of both students and parents, and parents will support you fully the rest of the year.

TECHNIQUE:

- Create a form such as the one below
- Notify parents as promptly as possible when you have "caught a student doing something good", either for you or another student, or improved his/her performance/behavior in some area

GUIDELINES:

I tried to "catch "every student at least once per quarter/grading period
You could accompany this with a Privilege Coupon trip to the treasure chest
Keep a copy for your records or the student's folder
It is also good to periodically send a list of recipients to the principal
Keep blank forms locked in a safe place, perhaps even in your department chair's or other teacher's room

GOOD DEED NOTIFICATION

Dear_____

(Student name)_____ was "caught"
doing the following god deed for

_____me

_____for another student

for _____

This occurred on _____(date)

In _____ (location)

_____
(teacher signature)

Good Deed performed: ---

MESSAGE:

Treasure Chest/Privilege Coupons

TIP: Using a Treasure Chest or Privilege Coupon for positive reinforcement

TECHNIQUE:
- create a "treasure chest" from a cardboard box or file box
- Decorate it or leave it plain, "it's what's inside that counts"
- Stock it with items such as the following: Privilege Coupons, small candies, (probably hard, some should be sugar-free), sugar-free gum, Re-do a Test or Assignment Coupon, pencils or pens, markers or highliters,etc.

TECHNIQUE: for Privilege Coupons
Create coupons using index cards or other heavy paper
Some privileges you could consider writing on the cards might be something like these:
1. Free tardy
2. Free food or gum day
3. Free pass (you may want to put on limitations)
4. Free late homework (must still be turned in, but could be a day late without penalty. My rule was that it could not be use for a presentation or other long-term or major assignment such as a research paper)

    5. Free trip to the treasure chest or piece of
       candy
    6. One early dismissal for lunch or after school

I recommend that you put your name and/or room
number on the back of the coupons in case they are left in
another room or area. You might also tell students they
should write their name on it These are like gold among
the students

- NOTE: These are only ideas, use them or not as fits
  your situation and comfort level. You can determine
  what is a privilege for your students.

- It may be a good idea to share these ides with your
  principal to get approval to use them as there may be
  specific rules or preferences about some of them
  about which you may not be aware. This is especially
  true of tardies, early dismissals, and passes.

- It is a good idea to require students to turn in the
  coupon when they use it that way there is no
  possibility of a second use or use by someone else.

- A Free Late homework coupon should probably be
  attached to the assignment to help you keep track of
  whether or not you should apply any late penalty to it

GUIDELINES:
Desirable behavior to reward might include these:
            Highest grade on a test
            Bringing all materials to class for a week

No missing homework for a specific amount of time (this is especially good for students who tend to be underachievers)

"Get item out of jail free"

Caution : avoid using "first one finished" as this will result in speed instead of quality as the object of the activity

(Sample Privilege Coupon)

_____

PRIVILEGE COUPON

This coupon is good for one late homework. You may turn in one regular assignment one day late without penalty (not good for oral presentation, or other long-term assignment).

Name _____

Assignment_____

Date Due_____

Date turned in _____

Problem Solving

TIP:
Problems
1. Students who don't bring materials to class
2. Students who leave items in your classroom

Solution:
Collect abandoned items at the end of the day/class, especially writing utensils.

- Put text books in "jail" until they are claimed
- Writing utensils: Keep in a cup/jar on your desk to loan to students who do not bring one
- Require some sort of "bail" for the release of abandoned items. This may include anything from donuts to a student ID card (for a short time). Sometimes I asked them to return a privilege card. You may even want to add a "get out of jail" card to your privilege cards.

GUIDELINES:
- Avoid using electronic devices as "bail"
- If a text book from another class is among the abandoned items, you may need to notify that teacher to determine the owner of the book

Absences

TIP: Keep a folder for work lists by absent students

TECHNIQUE:
- Keep a file folder on your desk for make-up work
- Tell students which folder serves that purpose
- When a student was absent I wrote his name on the top of any handouts or tests given that day in class
- It was then the student's responsibility to check the make-up folder for missed work

GUIDELINES:
- You may want to hand the student any tests missed when they return to class to avoid problems in using the folder.
- Student would need to arrange a time and a place to take the make-up tests, in some supervised situation that does not cause a problem for anyone

Appendix I: Weekly Evaluation Form

Name: _____ Grade: _____ Week of _____ to _____

Subject	Effort Grade	Behavior Grade	Weekly Grade	Week's Work Complete (Y/N)	Grade to Date	Teacher Signature
1						
2						
3						
4						
5						
6						
7						
8						
9						

Teacher Comments:

_____

_____

_____

_____

Please use the same rating for effort, behavior, and achievement:
A-Excellent   C-Average   F-Failing
B-Above Average   D-Below Average

Appendix II: Nine Famous People Who Blew It (But Later Made It Big)

Walt Disney: Once got fired by a newspaper editor because "He had no good ideas" He went on to create Mickey Mouse, Donald Duck, Disney Studios (which have won over 45 Academy Awards), Disneyland, Disneyworld; his greatest dream, EPCOT Center, opened in 1982.

Louisa May Alcott: Was told by an editor that she would never write anything popular. More than a century later, her novels are still being read. The Children's Literature Association considers Little Women one of the best American's children's books of the past two hundred years.

Madame Schumann Heink: Was told by an opera director that she would "never be a singer" that she should "buy a sewing machine." She went on to star in the Imperial Opera in Vienna.

Babe Ruth: Hit 714 home runs – but he also struck out 1,3390 times.

R. H. Macy: Failed seven times before making it big with his New York store.

Abraham Lincoln: Started out as a captain at the beginning of the Blackhawk War; by the end of the war, he had been demoted to private. He served as president of the United States.

Lee Iacocca: Was fired from Ford Motor Company by Henry Ford II. He designed the classic Ford Mustang. He later became chairman of the board at Chrysler and headed the campaign to restore the Statue of Liberty. (He even bought Henry Ford's old house and moved in.)

Thomas Edison: Teachers called him "Too stupid to learn." He made three thousand mistakes on his way to inventing the light bulb. Eventually he held 1093 patents.

John Creasey: English novelist, got 753 rejection slips before publishing the first of his 564 books.

Source: Elliott, Miriam Adderholdt Ph.D, Perfectionism: What's Bad About Being Too Good

Appendix III: General Notes and Hints from a Fifteen-year Veteran Teacher

Be flexible. There is always something to disrupt your plan for the day. These include:

> Assemblies
> Hearing and Vision screenings
> Picture days
> Pep Rallies
> Unscheduled department/team/faculty meetings
> Special staffings
> Early dismissal for major performances/sports events or rehearsals for those events
> Field trips for other classes - these are particularly troublesome since they usually involve only some of the students

Find out early the procedure for requesting transportation for field trips etc.

Consult your principal first for answers to questions you may have about school policies, then consult department chair persons.

Determine the policy for ordering supplies. These are sometimes stored with your department chair, so you may not need to order them. Be sure to anticipate projects which may require special supplies. There are some projects for which you should supply materials if they are unusual, and may be difficult for the average student to acquire.

Keep the students alert by occasionally doing unpredictable things such as:

Don't always start at the beginning of the alphabet or the front of the rows.

When reading aloud don't change readers with each paragraph, but change by sentence. Even when reading a drama/play it is just as effective to read by sentence rather than by parts.

Ascertain the school policy for "posting" grades. There may be legal issues about privacy.

Don't be afraid to admit if you don't know the answer to a student's question. Just tell them you will check on it and get back to them. This lets them know that it is okay for them to research their own answers.

Don't be afraid to modify your lesson/unit plans, or to take more time on a particular concept or a piece of literature.

Contact parents often, about positive issues as well as concerns. Parents appreciate all communication from school, especially if it's good news. Contact with parents is usually a good deterrent for future behavior problems.

Learn early in the year if it is okay to contact parents at their workplace and under what circumstances. This can be established by asking parents for phone numbers where they can be reached by sending home an index card or form.

Find out the library policy for sending a student to do research or homework for tests, and the counselors policy for seeing students for various reasons such as changing schedules and discussing problems.

Check with the principal about students journal entries that may indicate serious problems (abuse, violent tendencies, drug use, suicide or other dangerous behaviors). I always told my students that general entries were confidential unless they involved the wellbeing of themselves or others, or a legal issue.

Miscellaneous Tips

Don't always start at the top of the alphabet or the front of the room, go in reverse at rimes.

It is sometimes good to ask students to get up in front of the class at times other than for formal presentations. When you notice a student has grasped a concept, solved a difficult problem as you have circulated, ask him to explain his answer or theory to the class.. When a student raises his hand to answer a question, ask him to stand up ,even if just at his desk, to give the answer. This helps to dissuade fear of speaking in front of the class.

Have a student raise his hand to go first, then announce that the student to his right/left/opposite will actually be the one to start.

Attend students' extracurricular activities when possible, especially if you have more than one student in a particular activity. Then as they enter the classroom the next day, comment on his or the team's performance. This tells the student that you care about him as a student in and outside your class, and goes a long way in discouraging behavior problems, as well as boosting his self esteem. You can even involve the class in this by asking, "Who attended the _____ yesterday? Wasn't that a good _____?"

Also, don't be afraid to admit that you handled a behavior issue in a way other than you would have liked. Simply apologize and add that you're sorry you robbed him of a learning experience and that you will try to do things differently in the future. These two things let the student know that first of all, you are human, and secondly, that you are interested in improving yourself, and it encourages them to do the same.

Appendix IV: Extra-Curricular Experience

If you want to get even better acquainted with your students than just in your classroom, I would strongly suggest you consider getting involved in extra-curricular activities. There are many types of activities in which you could be of assistance.

Types of Activities

There are both academic and athletic areas for possible involvement. Athletic possibilities range from coach/assistant, scorekeeping, timing or officiating.

Specific opportunities include the following:

Academic

Forensics (competitive speech and debate)

> coach/assistance or critic

Matchwits (a trivia/knowledge bowl competition)

Athletic

Volleyball or baseball/softball scorekeeper

Track timer or start and finish judge

Football chain gang

Requirements

Many of these opportunities require no or minimal knowledge/experience in the activity.

Scorekeeping may require some knowledge or training; however, the coach is usually glad to provide training since he is happy to have your assistance.

Officials and critics training is often available through the state activities association or professional organizations.

Students or parents could be used in some of these areas; however, a faculty member lends credibility and fairness for participating teams.

Benefits

Most obvious is the respect and appreciation for your contribution by students, parents and colleagues.

Many schools/districts encourage or require extra curricular participation by the teaching staff. Stating you're willingness to get involved may give you an edge in competitive hiring.

Most schools offer a stipend for coaching/sponsoring activities. The amount of the stipend varies depending on length of the season or the number of performances, the number of students participating, and your experience.

In addition to a stipend, many activities have a per game/round pay scale, so your availability to work more than a single game/round could mean additional compensation.

Appendix V: Evaluation for Five Traits of Public Speaking

TRAIT	Positive Points (+)	Negative Points (-)	Points Earned	Points Possible
1. Organization	INTRO Topic was clearly given in a thesis sentence BODY Appropriate attention-getting device CONCLUSION Summarized main points	INTRO Topic was unclear or not stated at all BODY Too many or too few main points CONCLUSION Did not summarize		
2. Word Choice	All words used were grammatically correct and used correctly Words chosen were appropriate for the topic and easy to understand Words chosen were interesting	Used jargon or acronyms too often Words chosen were incorrect or used incorrectly		
3. Fluency	Used transitions to connect main points and "point the way" to the next point and were creative Main points followed each other appropriately	Used no transitions Jumped from one point to the next abruptly Transitions were ordinary and unimaginative (then, next, also) Main points did not connect appropriately		
4. Delivery	Used adequate and appropriate eye contact Posture was stable and appeared comfortable and confident Voice had appropriate volume and pacing Was clearly understood and used inflection to	Looked at the floor or at note cards too often Posture seemed unsteady, uncomfortable and uneasy, or used the "fig leaf" stance Voice was too much of a monotone Spoke too softly or too loudly Spoke too fast		

	make presentation sound interesting Facial expression conveyed interest and understanding and enthusiasm for topic Confidence Gestures seemed natural	Slurred words Looked bored with topic (yawning) Played with clothing or put hands into pockets Chewed gum Used interrupting phrases too often Rattled paper or note cards in a distracting way		
5. Visual Aid	Clearly visible from all areas of the room Speaker referred to it appropriately	Visual Aid was more of a distraction than an aid Speaker referred to it only rarely and in a jerky manner Was not visible to all Design and placement of aid forced speaker to turn his back to his audience		
Overall impression of speech	Fit within time frame Approached speaking area confidently Posture seemed natural			

NOTE: You can present a copy of this evaluation to students during the time you are teaching the concepts so they will know how they will be evaluated. You can circle the comments that fit the speaker instead of writing the comments out. If you allow five points per trait, it is easy to translate it into a percentage grade if that is your preference.

COMMENTS:

Conclusion

When I was a first time teacher, I was scared to death! Wisdom I would gain in the next fifteen years through experience, knowledge shared by other teachers, and information I acquired from several workshops and classes I attended, helped me gradually learn techniques that would decrease my fear and help me conduct a more interesting and effective class. I learned ways to handle discipline and classroom management by working in small groups and modifying my teaching methods to include all learning styles.

It is my hope that the information in this book will assist you in your teaching career.

Diana Skoog

My first year in Peyton